A Tribute to
Archbishop
Vincent Nichols

alive Publishing

Publisher to the Holy See

Published in 2009 by Alive Publishing Ltd.
Graphic House, 124 City Road,
Stoke on Trent ST4 2PH
Tel: +44 (0) 1782 745600
Fax: +44 (0) 1782 745500
www.alivepublishing.co.uk
e-mail: booksales@alivepublishing.co.uk

ISBN 978-1906278-01-4

CONTENTS

Photographer: **Sue Conway**

FOREWORD

Bishop William Kenney
Diocesan Administrator

It is a great honour and privilege for me to be invited to write the foreword to this tribute to Archbishop Vincent, celebrating, as it does, his time with us as our Archbishop.

I am grateful to everybody who has contributed to the tribute reflecting as they have done on their own experiences and memories of Archbishop Vincent during his time in the diocese.

I personally first came to know him when he was Secretary General to the Bishops' Conference and I was a new bishop in 1987. Since the end of 2006, when I was made an Auxillary Bishop by Pope Benedict, I have, of course, had contact with him several times a month.

I am immensely grateful to him for his warm welcome to me as I returned to the diocese after 37 years. Then, as I began to work here, it was a real pleasure to work with and for him as the Auxiliary Bishop responsible for the Southern Pastoral Region of the Diocese.

I have found him always kind and helpful, insightful about the various questions which arose and always with time to discuss whatever matters came up.

Each of the contributors has captured movingly and beautifully an insight, a dimension or an aspect of Archbishop Vincent's ministry as it has impacted or influenced their own department, organisation or simply their own lives.

Although all of them speak from their own perspective and as individuals, there is a way in which they also speak for us all, because what shines out from each tribute is the esteem, affection and indeed love both priests and people have for him.

On being appointed Archbishop of Westminster, Archbishop Vincent said: 'It is sad to be departing from the Archdiocese of Birmingham which I have learnt to appreciate, cherish and love. I will miss the priests and the people of the diocese very much indeed.' We too have learnt to appreciate, love and cherish him and we too will miss him very much indeed. ∎

William Bernard Ullathorne
A Different Kind of Monk

Judith Champ

Launch of *William Bernard Ullathorne, A Different Kind of Monk*, 2006
Photographer: **Sue Conway**

'HIS GIFT HAS
BEEN TO ENCOURAGE
US TO CHERISH AND
UNDERSTAND THE HISTORY
OF OUR DIOCESAN
COMMUNITY'

Judith Champ
Director of Studies
St Mary's College, Oscott

INSPIRED BY
ULLATHORNE

'There is one good thing about Archbishop Vincent leaving – at least we won't have to listen to your book being quoted any more! ' Words spoken to me recently by one of the priests of the diocese, which, I think, were intended humorously.

After many years of historical research, my biography of Ullathorne was published in 2006; it was seized on with relish by Archbishop Vincent, and used on many occasions. Anyone who has heard the Archbishop preach frequently will have picked up his appreciation for William Bernard Ullathorne, his first predecessor in Birmingham.

He drew inspiration from Ullathorne's deep and instinctive faith, his great care for the people and for the priests of the diocese, his encouragement of the vocations of women and his

fierce determination to advance the Mission of the Church in this area.

Archbishop Vincent came to Birmingham, like Ullathorne, as a relative stranger, yet, as he found his way around this huge and varied diocese, he began to absorb its history and tradition.

I know that over the past nine years, Archbishop Vincent has become steeped in that tradition and deeply appreciative of the roots of English Catholic life to be found in these Midland counties. We have talked often about the ways in which history has shaped the communities in which we now live, and on which the future of our local Church will be built.

Now, Archbishop Vincent's ministry here in Birmingham begins, sadly, to take its place in the history rather than the future of the diocese. That

will remain for future generations of historians to consider, but his immediate gift has been to encourage us all to cherish and understand the history of our diocesan community, and to integrate it into our present and future ministry.

Ullathorne was, of course, Newman's bishop and lifelong friend and ally, and we look forward to Archbishop Vincent leading national celebrations for the beatification and eventual canonisation of Newman in the not too distant future. So Ullathorne may yet be quoted in public again…! ∎

A CHRISTIAN CLASSIC

Maria Bracken
Sister of Andrew Robinson

My mum and dad met Archbishop Vincent nine years ago when he visited my brother Andrew Robinson at his home in Coventry. He was then a 4th year seminarian at Oscott College and had just been diagnosed with cancer.

My mum remembers hearing them chatting and laughing together in the front room and Andrew told her that the Archbishop had asked him to write a journal of his experience. This was an inspired request from the Archbishop, as the journal Andrew wrote was a deeply moving account of what were to be the last months of his life.

Tears at Night, Joy at Dawn can be read in one sitting, so many readers

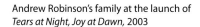

> I REMEMBER SEEING THE
> ARCHBISHOP KNEEL AT
> ANDREW'S BEDSIDE
> AS HE PRAYED AND
> SAID HIS GOODBYE

bedside as he prayed and said his goodbye. He touched my face as he left, and in his eyes I remember seeing such compassion and love it moved me to tears.

The Archbishop is the patron of the Andrew Robinson Young People's Trust, the legacy left behind as a tribute to the work Andrew started in his life. This work has been continued through sales of *Tears at Night, Joy at Dawn*.

Many young people have received such a positive experience of our loving Church through the work of this trust, and we owe such a debt of gratitude for the love and support we have received from Archbishop Vincent. Westminster is so very lucky to have been sent such a truly great man. ■

tell me, and has been the source through which many people have come to know our Lord in a very real way. Without the wisdom and insight of Archbishop Vincent, *Tears at Night, Joy at Dawn* would never have been written and it has given much inspiration, comfort and joy to his friends and family to know some good has come from Andrew's death.

In March 2001 the Archbishop saw Andrew at the dedication of the statue of Our Lady of Coventry. Amongst all the people and dignitaries gathered, he made time to stop and chat with Andrew, this we know meant a lot to him. The next time we saw Archbishop Vincent was at Andrew's bedside. He had heard Andrew had only a few hours left to live and had rushed to be there, but Andrew died minutes before he arrived.

I remember after all the thousands of prayers that had been said for Andrew whether a miracle would happen right at the last moment, but it was not to be. I remember seeing the Archbishop kneel at Andrew's

Dr Pat Crosby
Medical Director
Lourdes Pilgrimage

'HIS ATTENTION TO
THE SICK DURING
A BUSY WEEK IS
REMARKABLE; HE
REALLY IS HANDS ON'

PILGRIM WITH THE SICK

Archbishop Vincent's first visit with the Diocesan Lourdes Pilgrimage was in May 2000. He has held a keen interest in the pilgrimage since then and has come every year to be on pilgrimage with us. His attention to the sick during a busy week is remarkable; he really is 'hands on', visiting the ward every day, sometimes several times; asking the doctors about diagnoses and medical problems which arise during the course of the pilgrimage and asking to be kept updated and informed.

A few years ago Kitty, one of our elderly pilgrims, went into heart failure at the airport as we were coming home. Archbishop Vincent was immediately informed and, as I was giving her an intravenous injection, he came up calmly beside me. After I had given the injection he blessed and anointed her. To this day

Kitty credits Archbishop Vincent with her survival and not the intravenous injection!

I have so many fond memories which come flooding back because he was always so active and involved in the pilgrimage. He even has the accolade of being described as a 'Hoodie'. He has been seen at various events on the pilgrimage wearing the sweat top of various organizations and schools: the Birmingham Catholic Youth Association (BCYS), Blessed George Napier School, the Too Old to Be Young (TOBY) group and, last year, Bishop Walsh School. He certainly has a fashionable selection to choose from.

Philip, a friend of the Archbishop, has travelled as one of the sick pilgrims each year. Sometimes he can become restless and agitated and when he gets into this state it can be hard to

calm or console him. Archbishop Vincent is then called and he brings with him a bag carrying his vestments. Philip then guards the bag, and immediately settles down and calm and peace is restored!

Philip was present at the Archbishop's Installation in Westminster as was Fr Gerry Breen, the Pilgrimage Director. I like to think of them being there carrying the prayers and love of the patients, pilgrims and all the carers of the sick, for our Archbishop Vincent of whom we are so proud and to whom we are so grateful for the time he gave us. ■

Picture by Yvonne Belfield
St Augustine's School, Birmingham

'THE CATHOLIC SCHOOLS
IN OUR DIOCESE HAVE
MUCH TO THANK
ARCHBISHOP VINCENT
FOR DURING HIS TIME AS
OUR BISHOP'

Fr Marcus Stock
Director of Schools

A CATHOLIC VISION

From day one, Archbishop Vincent has actively supported the work of the Diocesan Schools Commission in all its dimensions.

This has been expressed through the provision of resources for new school buildings and facilities; by encouraging the work of foundation governors to maintain and develop the fundamental partnership between schools and the diocese. Also his support has been unstinting in promoting high quality Catholic school leadership; and through strengthening the Catholic ethos in diocesan schools and their foundation in the values of the gospel.

Over the last nine years, Archbishop Vincent's support for Catholic Education has been rooted in a clear understanding of the issues and the challenges which the diocese has faced in maintaining the provision of Catholic schools.

In giving leadership, he has combined considerable intellectual capacity with great pastoral sensitivity. This means that, in the development of policy and strategy, a genuine concern for individuals and communities has never been lost sight of or forgotten.

Perhaps the best tribute I can pay is to the simplicity of the priest and pastor at the core of the Archbishop's ministry which has shone through in his visits to schools.

I remember being at one of the Archbishop's visits to a primary school and witnessing him sitting in the middle of the school hall surrounded by all the children; he was teaching them to sing a simple prayer-song:

'Be a rock of refuge for me, O Lord. Be a rock of refuge for me'. In a profound way that scene captured the essence of why the Church provides Catholic schools – to enable our young people to develop joyful lives of prayerful intimacy with the Lord and to grow, without fear, to their full potential in the knowledge and love of God.

The Catholic schools in our diocese have much to thank Archbishop Vincent for during his time as our bishop. I know that his ministry here will be very much missed by those schools but he goes to Westminster assured of their prayers for his future. ■

Special Mass to celebrate 40th anniversary of Newman University College, 2008
Photographer: **Peter Jennings**

'I SAY', SAID MY CONTACT, 'THAT
ARCHBISHOP OF YOURS; HE'S REALLY
SOMETHING ELSE, ISN'T HE. I'VE
NEVER HEARD A BETTER DEFENCE
OF ACADEMIC FREEDOM!'.

Pamela Taylor
Principal
Newman University College

FAITH AND REASON UNITE

When Archbishop Vincent arrived in Birmingham, he acquired a wide range of additional responsibilities; one of these was to be the Chair of the Board of Governors at what was then Newman College of Higher Education.

Over the years Archbishop Vincent has supported us and our students by presiding at the Mass and awards ceremony for those receiving the Catholic Certificate in Religious Studies. He has attended our Graduation Ceremonies in Symphony Hall, impressing the Chancellor of the University of Leicester so much that the University awarded him an Honorary Doctorate. Archbishop Vincent has led staff development sessions for staff and governors as well as presiding at special Masses such as our 40th Anniversary Mass. He has made himself available, has offered wise counsel and has brought humour, kindness and warmth to his role and to our University College.

Perhaps his most important contribution came during the time when the College was assessed for Taught Degree Awarding Powers. After a year long inspection period, the Quality Assurance Agency came to their very last meeting with the Governors. That morning a negative story had broken about another Church University constraining a particular development and the media were asking if universities with a Christian foundation could really provide academic freedom.

Our assessors asked the Archbishop this question. His answer was deeply impressive, stressing the absolute freedom that came from faith in God and the moral obligation to interrogate ideas in the light of that truth. His argument for the importance of universities being places where Faith and Reason came together to enable human beings to get closer to Truth was inspiring. We achieved our Taught Degree Awarding Powers and became Newman University College.

Afterwards, I was contacted by someone from the Quality Assurance Agency who had been in the room and heard the Archbishop. 'I say', said my contact, 'that Archbishop of yours; he's really something else, isn't he. I've never heard a better defence of academic freedom!'

Well, we thought he was 'something else' too and all at Newman will miss him. But we were equally delighted that he has been chosen to lead the Catholic community in England and we look forward to his continued influence. ■

Fr Paul Chavasse

Postulator for the Cause of Cardinal
Newman - The Oratory, Birmingham

PROMOTING NEWMAN'S CAUSE

When Archbishop Vincent came to Birmingham in March 2000, I think it true to say that he was not particularly well-versed in the situation regarding Cardinal Newman's Cause for Beatification. There was no reason that he should have been!

But how quickly that was to change! It had to, as a diocesan bishop is by the nature of things intimately involved in the procedures surrounding a Cause's progress, even when that Cause (like Newman's) is not of a diocesan priest.

Several factors combined to achieve this change. In 2001 Pope John Paul II issued a Letter to commemorate the bi-centenary of Cardinal Newman's birth, and that was addressed directly to Archbishop Vincent.

Then, soon after, news began to arrive of a possible cure through Newman's intercession and, once again, the Archbishop was closely involved as matters moved forward, firstly in Boston, where the cure took place, and then in Rome as the Vatican officials examined what had happened.

All of this led Archbishop Vincent to become really interested in, and supportive of, the Cause. He gave most generously of his time and energy, and was always ready to assist with practical help – whether dealing with media interest, financial concerns, conspiracy theorists (not a few of those!) or even the writing of prayers! We owe him a great debt of gratitude for all of this.

Archbishop Vincent took particular interest in all the events of last autumn which surrounded the opening of the Cardinal's grave and the exhumation of its contents, and showed that great care and attention to detail which are so much the hallmark of the man. Cardinal Newman's Cause is bigger than the Birmingham Oratory, bigger than our Archdiocese; it is something the benefit of the universal Church. Even though, as Archbishop of Westminster, Archbishop Vincent will no longer be the bishop most closely involved, I know he will continue to show an active interest as the Cause continues to progress. ■

Photographer: **Sue Conway**

'ARCHBISHOP VINCENT TOTALLY EMBRACED THE PERMANENT DIACONATE AS A VITAL MINISTRY IN THE MODERN CHURCH'

Fr Paul Chamberlain
Director of Permanent Diaconate

EMBRACING THE PERMANENT DIACONATE

Coming from Liverpool Archbishop Vincent had been a priest of a diocese which was the first to embrace the Permanent Diaconate after it was re-established by Pope Paul VI. However, after he had been appointed as secretary to the Bishop's Conference, and later as an auxiliary bishop in Westminster, he had worked in a diocese where the Permanent Diaconate had not been introduced. He came then to Birmingham with very little recent experience of the Permanent Diaconate and maybe shared some of his late mentor, Cardinal Hume's, hesitations about it.

When he appointed me as Director, I felt we were both on a steep learning curve about this ministry. At that stage the Formation of Permanent Deacons was at Maryvale, but we both felt the more appropriate place would be at Oscott, where those under formation could be formed alongside the priests of the diocese and experience the great formation tradition that is Oscott.

He knew that anyone in ministry needed to be well equipped to deal with the issues of modern life, and so the formation programme was increased from three to four years. We shall be ordaining our first batch of students formed at Oscott in July 2009.

He encouraged me to create a Handbook for the Permanent Diaconate in the diocese which codified practice for the Permanent Diaconate in the diocese, clarifying issues relating to priests and deacons working together. In it, describing his vision for the diaconate, he wrote: 'Every parish might strive to have a deacon, thus establishing across the diocese a network of deacons whose task would be to build up the presence and activity of the Church in the service of the poor.' Archbishop Vincent totally embraced the Permanent Diaconate as a vital ministry in the modern Church.

When the news came through that Archbishop Vincent had been appointed to Westminster, I was giving a retreat at Knock to the first year of students studying for the diaconate in Ireland. I felt both devastated and elated. Devastated that we, and I personally, had lost a strong but gentle Archbishop who was always warm and welcoming, willing to listen and give time and be supportive of the work he had given me to do; elated, because his appointment to Westminster meant that the Church in this country had the man needed to lead it during this time of militant secularism. ∎

GRATITUDE FOR THE ELDERLY

Sr Francis
Little Sisters of the Poor, St Joseph's,
Harborne

I n the year 2000 a National Mass was celebrated in the National Exhibition Centre to celebrate the Millennium. It was a wonderful occasion, and just before the beginning of the processions Archbishop Vincent Nichols was being interviewed by the media. He had only recently arrived in Birmingham, after having worked for several years with Cardinal Basil Hume who had died in 1999. The inevitable question was asked him: 'What was Cardinal Hume like?' After a moment's reflection the answer came 'He was lovely'.

At St Joseph's some of our residents are sick, infirm and elderly clergy – our mission is to take care of them.

Archbishop Vincent celebrates Mass at St Joseph's Nursing Home, Harborne on Christmas Eve, 2005
Photographer: **Peter Jennings**

ARCHBISHOP VINCENT HAS A GREAT RESPECT AND GRATITUDE FOR THE ELDERLY PRIESTS WHO ARE NOW RETIRED FROM ACTIVE SERVICE

We here at St Joseph's are very grateful to Archbishop Vincent and thank him from our hearts for sharing our lives during the few years that he spent with us. There are so many things that he did for us in helping us to draw closer to God. We were truly blest! He can be always certain that our love and prayers are with him in this huge task that has been entrusted to him.

In the process of writing this tribute and casting my mind back to those media interviews which greeted him when he came to Birmingham in 2000 I found myself asking, 'What is Archbishop Vincent like?' All I can say is: 'We think he is lovely!' ■

Archbishop Vincent has a very special place in his heart for all his brother priests and has a great respect and gratitude for the elderly priests who are now retired from active service and are being cared for themselves. I saw this myself personally many times but every Christmas Eve morning Archbishop Vincent would pay a visit to us at Harborne. He came to concelebrate Mass with the six retired priests who lived here. After the Mass Archbishop Vincent would go on a visit of the entire house and speak to each person, resident and member of staff, before having lunch with the priests. He has a remarkable ability to make everybody feel special and valued, and there was never any sense of him being in a hurry or impatient to go elsewhere. His visit was a real high spot for St Joseph's and very much appreciated by all.

Fr Gerry Breen is made Honorary Chaplain to the Lourdes Shrine and is presented with his cross of office by Archbishop Vincent
Photographer: **Sue Conway**

Fr Gerry Breen
Pilgrimage Director

> 'HE WAS A DAILY VISITOR TO THE ACCUEIL HOSPITAL VISITING OUR SICK PILGRIMS AND OTHERS'

A LOURDES PILGRIM

Shortly after his arrival in the diocese Archbishop Vincent preached a sermon to the clergy of the diocese of which the main message was: Christ first in all things. These words were the mandate for his ministry amongst us.

He joined his first Birmingham Diocesan Pilgrimage to Lourdes rather late, following the Mass for the Jubilee at the National Exhibition Centre. His characteristic humour and ease endeared him to all regardless of age or indeed football affiliation! He insisted on time in the week to address our young people personally and to give each some token as a reminder of their pilgrimage.

He was a daily visitor to the Accueil Hospital visiting our Sick Pilgrims and others. He could also always be seen out and about in the Town and Sanctuary greeting and meeting people. His great strength is that he is both approachable and accessible to all our pilgrims. Our annual Clergy Evening was always an occasion for enjoyment and encouragement.

The Year 2008, marking the 150th Anniversary of the Apparitions, was to be his last with us. Our annual pilgrimage represents the greatest coming together of the diocese, and 2008 proved to be a bumper year with more than 2000 Birmingham Pilgrims in Lourdes, including 54 clergy.

Our joint Podium Mass, for English Speaking Pilgrims, attracted almost 6000. Archbishop Vincent preached an animated homily, assisted by 30 of our youngsters who stood in 3 groups of ten around the altar holding individual cards that spelled out the word: PILGRIMAGE. Specific cards were raised or lowered to spell out the words: PIL AGE and GRIM .

It was a difficult year with restrictions on numbers and on the availability of beds and hotels. Many did not get what they had hoped for and there were one or two moans and groans!

Archbishop Vincent suggested that many of us may be feeling GRIM because of the overcrowding, etc.. However, the alternative: PILAGE is the way of a world where Christ is not the centre. Alternatively, he suggested, GRIM could mean: 'Grace Received through Immaculate Mary? The choice was ours!

We are very grateful for all that he has given to the diocese and the pilgrimage, and we shall certainly miss him. Our prayer is for Our Lady of Lourdes to continue to watch over him as he continues his ministry in Westminster. If Christ is first in all things then, in him, we are never far from each other! ∎

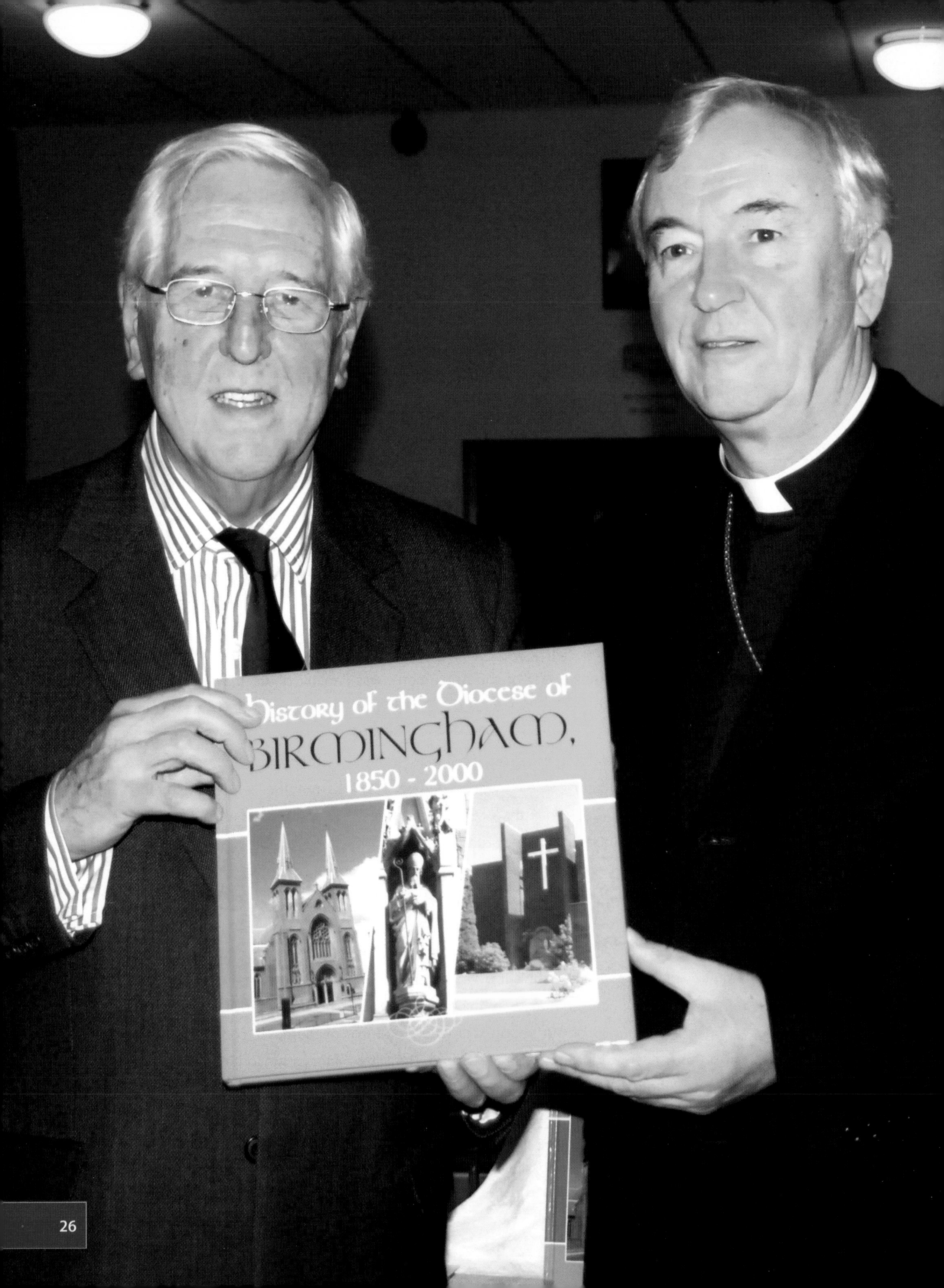
History of the Diocese of
BIRMINGHAM,
1850 - 2000

Launch of *History of the Diocese of Birmingham*, 2008
Photographer: **Sue Conway**

> 'HE HAS GONE TO
> WESTMINSTER AT
> AN EXTRAORDINARY,
> PROVIDENTIAL MOMENT IN
> OUR NATIONAL HISTORY'

Jack Scarisbrick
Historical Commission

A GIFTED COMMUNICATOR

I t was inevitable that he would go. But that does not make the parting any easier for us.

A stranger when he came to Birmingham nine years ago, he quickly appreciated two things: the richness of our Catholic heritage and the fact that the diocese was in good heart - thanks, above all, to his predecessor.

Archbishop Vincent has had the wisdom not to embark on major changes but to allow what he inherited to flourish. A natural leader, he has given us new confidence. We have been proud of him. He is modern and approachable – but keeps a necessary distance. A gifted communicator, he is exceptionally sure-footed with the media.

Most importantly, his concern for our spiritual life, evidenced, for example, by his *Walk with Me* programme, has been untiring. He has been good for us. We hope we have been good for him! He has returned to familiar territory – and to take on a huge new job.

He knows what we face, because he confronted it here: militant secularism, the rampant sex industry (abetted by much of the media), an often brutal, nihilistic popular culture, a lamentable loss of respect for human life, and so on. But he has gone to Westminster at an extraordinary, providential moment in our national history.

In the past few months we have been engulfed by a sudden near-cataclysmic global financial crisis. Then, in the past few days, we have discovered that parliament, the

political heart of the nation, is riddled by the same reckless greed that has nearly brought our economy to its knees. All this is shocking and bewildering.

It is also salutary. Who can now deny that our society needs to examine its collective conscience? Who can now be sure that the relentless anti-life and anti-Christian legislation of recent decades was as righteous as many claimed?

Here is a unique opportunity for the Catholic Church to give moral leadership to this country, to heal our society's brokenness, to liberate it from its godlessness and to bring the light of Christ to dispel its darkness. Westminster's new archbishop could indeed be its greatest. ∎

Photographer: **Sue Conway**

> HE WAS ALWAYS WILLING TO MEET VICTIMS.
> HE NEVER STOOD ON CEREMONY BUT MADE
> THEM FEEL AT EASE, POURING THE TEA,
> CHATTING ABOUT THE FOOTBALL RESULTS
> OR COMMENTING ON A PICTURE.

Jane Jones
Child Protection Officer

SAFEGUARDING AND PROTECTING

Many people will have seen Archbishop Vincent presiding at wonderful Masses, resplendent in vestments and mitre. Few will be aware of the important work he did to address the difficult and sensitive issue of abuse.

My first opportunity to work with Archbishop Vincent came not too long after he arrived in Birmingham. At that time cases of abuse by priests were very much in the headlines. I was part of a group of people who looked at existing guidelines in the light of the newly published Nolan Report.

The Archbishop attended every meeting and went through all the details with us. Then, when a properly structured national system came into being, Archbishop Nichols was given a key role it its management.

The result is that there is now a transparent system for responding to allegations of abuse in the Catholic Church which is recognised by the police and other agencies. Keeping children and vulnerable adults safe in our parishes is, of course, the most important consideration.

This is a demanding task largely achieved though the efforts of lay representatives. Last autumn Archbishop Vincent said Mass for, and spent the day with, people from all over the diocese who work so hard to keep our parishes safe. It was a wonderful event.

Those who have been hurt by abuse must always be the main focus of concern. Some people are helped if what has happened to them is acknowledged by a representative of the Church.

The Archbishop was always willing to meet victims. He never stood on ceremony but made them feel at ease, pouring the tea, chatting about the football results or commenting on a picture. He gently allowed them to say the things that they needed to say, and encouraged them to take whatever action would be helpful in their unique circumstance.

Being able to relate easily and genuinely to all sorts of people is a rare and wonderful gift; now it will be shared even more widely. ■

FORMING YOUNG
HEARTS AND MINDS

Fr Jonathan Veasey
Diocesan Director of
Religious Education

'When we look to Christ we discover the real truth about ourselves and what it means to be human.' Archbishop Vincent has so often made this remark when addressing teachers and those engaged in the work of Catholic education in our diocese.

For me, it summarises his commitment to the educational mission of our schools, which has been outstanding. His teaching and pastoral leadership have helped all those involved in the life and work of our schools to focus their attention on the person of Christ as the foundation of our educational mission. This has helped all of us think beyond the parameters of the

Department of Religious Education Advisory Team at the launch of Prayer Bags for Primary Schools, held at St Thomas More Primary School, Sheldon, May 2009
Photographer: **Sue Conway**

'HE HAS REMINDED TEACHERS TO BE WITNESSES TO CHRIST.'

contemporary education system and recognise that Catholic education is at its best when it is at the service of faith and the best interests of the human person. Archbishop Vincent has been constant in his support for the work of the Department of Religious Education.

Soon after arriving in Birmingham, he launched our new curriculum strategy for religious education in primary schools, encouraging teachers to take every opportunity to teach the Catholic faith and provide our children and young people with

the best opportunities to learn from it. In the many addresses he has made to teachers and governors and through visits to schools and parishes, he has always reaffirmed the importance he attaches to young people's seeking and discovering the truth about Christ, understanding how that impacts upon their lives as individuals, their belonging to the Church and their contribution to the world in which they live.

Archbishop Vincent has regularly met with groups of teachers from around the diocese to reflect with

them about aspects of our Catholic faith and mission. He has encouraged us to see the essential contribution that Catholic education makes to creating a cohesive society. He has reminded teachers to be witnesses to Christ and people of prayer and to contribute towards the formation of young people for the Church of tomorrow. This work has helped many teachers to develop a better understanding of their vocation and filled them with zeal for their work.

Archbishop Vincent leaves us with much to learn from and build upon. For this we will be forever grateful and we offer our prayerful support in the many new tasks that are now ahead of him. ■

A Tribute to Archbishop Vincent Nichols

'BUT THE WORKING DAY
WAS ALWAYS A HAPPY ONE.
ARCHBISHOP VINCENT
HAS AN EXCELLENT SENSE
OF HUMOUR AND LOVES A
GOOD JOKE.'

Jennifer Davies
Archbishop Vincent's Secretary
2000 - 2009

A GREAT BOSS AND FRIEND

One evening nine years ago I received a phone call at home from Archbishop Couve de Murville's Clerical Secretary, advising me that the new Archbishop of Birmingham would be announced the next day and that he would be coming to Birmingham in readiness for this. It was all very exciting, but a little daunting at the same time. The next day I met Archbishop Vincent for the first time and it was the start of a very happy and memorable nine years.

Archbishop Vincent is a hard worker and we were certainly kept busy. I often thought of sabotaging his dictation machine! But the working day was always a happy one. Archbishop Vincent has an excellent sense of humour and loves a good joke. The only down side was having to listen about football from time to time, especially if a big match

was going to be on. It didn't take Archbishop Vincent long to realise that I had no interest whatsoever in 'the beautiful game' although he persevered, relentlessly – but without success!

Thanks to Archbishop Vincent I have taken part in, some very special and memorable events. Some nicer than others! Despite being frightened of heights, I recently took part in a tandem skydive organised by *Catholic Today* to raise much needed money for the Johnson Fund, which takes care of the sick, elderly and infirm secular priests of the diocese.

When I was first approached by *Catholic Today* and asked if I would be interested in taking part I mentioned it to the Archbishop. 'Oh, you must!' was his reply – which was a little too eager for my liking!

I was deeply honoured recently when the Archbishop asked me to read at his Mass of Installation at Westminster Cathedral on 21 May. I felt so very privileged. It was a wonderful occasion and a memory I will treasure.

I, and all the staff at Archbishop's House, will miss the Archbishop immensely. I know he will do a first class job in Westminster. I also know that despite being very busy he will always be approachable and that, although we won't see or speak to him often, we won't lose touch entirely. ■

'THE BIRMINGHAM
FAITH LEADERS
GROUP BENEFITTED
FROM ARCHBISHOP
VINCENT'S WISE AND
REALISTIC INFLUENCE'

David Urquhart
Bishop of Birmingham

CO-WORKING FOR THE GOSPEL

Just three years ago, on the announcement of my appointment as Bishop of Birmingham in May 2006, I walked into St Philip's Cathedral to be greeted by the Faith Leaders Group, amongst whom was Archbishop Vincent.

His welcome to me, and our partnership in the gospel across the city of Birmingham, remained steadfast throughout the remainder of his time here.

A generosity of access, prayer and friendship, coupled with a love for Christian truth and the common good, marked his commitment to our work together.

Whether speaking out on national, social and educational issues, paying attention to resolving tensions and misunderstandings in local communities, or ensuring the continuity of parish and chaplaincy ministry, there was a strong sense of co-operation.

The distinctiveness of Church schools, the particular contribution to family life of Catholic adoption agencies, support for reconciliation in gang or terror related incidents, and the securing of a Faith Centre in the new Queen Elizabeth Hospital all focussed our minds and actions.

As Presidents, with the Free Church Moderator, of Birmingham Churches Together, we were able to support a new way of structuring ecumenical witness and action. There is a renewed emphasis in shared ministry and mission with the Council of Black-led Churches.

The Birmingham Faith Leaders Group, bringing together the six main religions of Birmingham, Christians, Muslims, Jews, Sikhs, Hindus and Buddhists, benefitted from Archbishop Vincent's wise and realistic influence. In their writing for the local press and in collaborating with the Local Authority and University in the 'Faiths for the City' seminars, group members aimed at building a good city from their own religion's distinctive positions and beliefs.

Most memorable of all was the recent Walk of Witness on Good Friday and seeing the Cross of Christ held high as we followed behind, walking through Birmingham's New Street linking the city centre, Council House, St Philip's and finally to pray together the Stations of the Cross in St Chad's Cathedral.

I am sure we shall continue as co-workers in the gospel in the two great cities of London and Birmingham. ■

THE CHRISTIAN LEADER

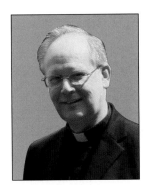

Fr John Carlyle
Diocesan Treasurer

Archbishop's Council 2009
Photographer: **Peter Jennings**

When I was still new as Diocesan Treasurer, I met Archbishop Vincent at a conference. He was Auxiliary Bishop in Westminster then, and was acting as link between the Diocesan Financial Secretaries and the Bishops' Conference. The long day had been going well when Bishop Nichols happened to take a seat directly in front of me.

At the end of that session he turned round and greeted me, welcoming me warmly and with an apology that he had not done so earlier. I was somewhat taken aback by this. In the thrusting, ambitious, commercial world, in which I had spent most of my early adult life, I had found that such a humble, apologetic greeting might happen sometimes, but very rarely. The warmth of that encounter stayed with me.

The last occasion on which most priests of this diocese met the Archbishop was at Mass in the Cathedral the day before he left for London. His homily was full of praise for all that is good in our diocese.

He alluded to himself and his future mainly in abstract terms, and in the light of that day's readings. His most personal note was to ask forgiveness for whatever hurt he had caused in his time here. It was a humble, apologetic farewell.

Now, it is the nature of leadership that a leader will, in the normal course of things, occasionally, and unintentionally, give offence. It can hardly be avoided. The traps are everywhere. But it was typical of Archbishop Vincent that he should be more concerned for the feelings of those present than for his own dignity.

You remember a person for how you felt when you left their presence. Archbishop Vincent was always concerned to see to it that one left him feeling positive about things, even if he had had to ask or say something difficult. That was his way.

The day after that final Mass a removal van arrived outside Archbishop's House. The name of the firm was ironically - *Bishops Move*! Sadly, they do; though sometimes one might wish they didn't. ■

> HIS MOST PERSONAL NOTE WAS TO ASK FORGIVENESS FOR WHATEVER HURT HE HAD CAUSED IN HIS TIME HERE. IT WAS A HUMBLE, APOLOGETIC FAREWELL.

Chrism Mass 2009
Photographer: Sue Conway

A Shepherd's Heart

Kevin Caffrey
Director
Fr Hudson's Society

Top: Fr Hudson's Ball 2007
Photographer: **Sue Conway**
Right: Father Hudson's Bike Ride.
Photographer: **Peter Jennings**

As I write this short reflection we are about to embark upon the annual Good Shepherd Masses when our schools bring the results of their Lenten Fundraising activities in support of the work of the Society.

Prior to the arrival of Archbishop Vincent to Birmingham the tradition had been a single Mass either at Coleshill or the Cathedral with around 20 schools attending. This year we have Masses in seven locations throughout the diocese and each will be packed with school children praying and singing their hearts out. The difference is due directly to the encouragement and support of Archbishop Vincent, and for me this typically sums up his time as Archbishop of Birmingham.

He carried out his role as President of the Society most seriously and took great interest in its growing work throughout the diocese. Over the years we shared some difficult issues together, including the historical abuse claims and, latterly, the impact of the Sexual Orientation Regulations on our Adoption services, but in all

these he was always available for discussion, advice, encouragement and ready to provide clear leadership in a way that left me inspired and feeling supported.

I am left with many happy memories of his involvement with and visits to Coleshill which include the Blessing of our new Offices in 2000, his presiding over the 100th Meeting of the Society's Council of Trustees in December 2006, and his participation in the fund-raising Bike Rides. The Hudson Way ride, held last year (2008), included a stop-off at the home of Richard Hudson. Here we met up with the relations of our Founder, Father George Hudson. It was a most enjoyable occasion when the Archbishop addressed us all and kindly invited me to say a few words.

Archbishop Vincent in all his dealings was very warm and personable. For example, he would ring me up at home on occasions and thus often speak to my wife, Maria, who three years ago had major surgery on her spine leaving her with mobility difficulties. His words of encouragement to her and, in particular, I quote, 'Be gentle with yourself', have been wonderfully healing for us both.

I wrote to him recently thanking him for all of his encouragement and support and finished by saying 'We will miss you here in Birmingham' – what more could I say? ∎

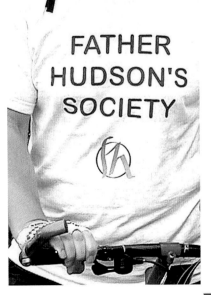

THE GIFT OF PRIESTHOOD

Mgr Mark Crisp
Rector
St Mary's College, Oscott

St Mary's College Oscott **2009**
Photographer: **Peter Harrington**

O n May 9th, Archbishop Vincent Nichols made his last visit as Archbishop of Birmingham to this seminary at Oscott. With so much on his mind, he might have been excused for merely turning up to say goodbye. Instead, he asked if he could join the community in prayer and give a talk to the students, in which he explored the reality of answering God's call in the life of a priest. In doing this, he demonstrated, yet again, the deep concern he always showed for seminarians throughout his time in the diocese.

At the special dinner that followed, the Dean of Students, Michael Collis, thanked him for the encouragement

he has always given to those who feel that they are called to priesthood, particularly today when so often, in society, people try to deter anyone who feels this call.

It would be fair to say, therefore, that the most significant contribution he made at Oscott was his care to foster the gift of priesthood.

In this sense, he lived up to his predecessor and hero, Bishop Ullathorne, first bishop of Birmingham, who said that the seminary should be 'as the Church intends, the family of the bishop, in which he will take singular interest, and over which he will exercise a singular care; to which his whole heart will be given.'

His care for Oscott, however, was not domineering or interfering. He has a great capacity for entrusting responsibility to others and then allowing them to be creative and develop initiatives in their own way.

I know I can speak on behalf of all the formation staff and say that, given the strength of his support and his clear vision of priesthood, we have been able to enjoy our work as formators under his care.

We are sad to see him leave us but we are confident that in his new role he will give clear leadership and vision regarding the importance of the priesthood in the evangelisation of our nation.

In this way, we know that he will, even from a distance, still foster vocations to the priesthood way beyond the confines of the Archdiocese of Westminster. ■

> 'HE IS NOT
> JUST A MAN OF
> WORDS BUT A MAN OF
> ACTION'

Maria Bracken
Birmingham Catholic Youth Service

A MAN OF ACTION

I always thought I was reasonably fit, jogged round the park, swam at the local pool, but it wasn't until I joined the volunteers taking part in Cycle for Youth that that theory was blown out of the water!

I remember making my way with gritted teeth up a steep hill in the Malverns. I was concentrating on breathing and trying to keep a steady rhythm going when who should come cycling past me but our 63-year-old Archbishop!

He was not just peddling faster than I, I might add, but chatting as he rode! Even though he left me for dust you cannot help but be inspired by Archbishop Vincent.

Without his fund-raising support and the way that he has raised the profile of the Birmingham Catholic Youth Service, the diocese would have lost a most valuable resource. We have been so blessed in our diocese to have been sent our Archbishop if only for a short while. His support has meant that new parish youth groups have opened up and many parish volunteers have been trained.

His support has meant that events both local and diocesan have been created, enabling young people from our parishes to come together and celebrate what it means to be a young Catholic.

Pilgrimages led by the Archbishop to Lourdes and World Youth Day have had strong dynamic young representatives from across the Archdiocese of Birmingham.

Our Archbishop trained and rode through hail, rain and sunshine. He battled bigger hills than me and long stretches of open road, and why? - because the young people of this diocese are important to him.

He is not just a man of words but a man of action. He made every effort to speak to all those taking part in Cycle for Youth and, when he did, that person felt a part of something bigger than themselves, they felt included, important and part of a community, and that is what our Church is about.

He will be sorely missed, but we wish him all our love and prayers and thanks as he goes on to serve the people of Westminster. ■

THE CHIEF CATECHIST

Mgr Paul J Watson
Director of Maryvale Institute

Graduation day 2005
Photographer: **Ede & Ravenscroft**

'The Bishop is the Chief Catechist of the Diocese'. As Maryvale was established as a Catechetical Institute in the Archdiocese of Birmingham, the Institute's work and mission is a participation and extension of the catechetical mission and office of the Bishop.

When Vincent Nichols became the Archbishop of Birmingham he also

THE TIME OF
THE ARCHBISHOP'S
PRESIDENCY HAS BEEN
A TIME OF GROWTH
AND DEVELOPMENT FOR
MARYVALE.

of the various degree programmes, Archbishop Vincent has recognised and strongly encouraged the place of Maryvale within the world of Higher Education in our country, especially when he presided over the annual Degree Ceremony in the Cathedral.

He has been keen for us to maintain our strong link with the Open University Validation Services, while at the same time supporting the Diocese and the parishes in catechetical formation.

The time of the Archbishop's presidency has been a time of growth and development for Maryvale. We are immensely grateful for the lead Archbishop Vincent has given in facilitating negations with the Congregation for Catholic Education in Rome, which are leading, hopefully in the very near future, to the recognition in Rome of Maryvale as an Ecclesiastical Institute.

Our best tribute to our President will be to continue to follow the course and the principles he emphasised. Our prayers go with him in his future ministry and work. ■

became the President of Maryvale and the Chair of both the Trustees and General Council. I remember his first visit to the Institute, which was in the year before I took up the role of Director. I was still learning about the responsibilities of the Director as well as coming to grips with the world of Higher Education, Validating Bodies, the methodology of Distance Learning and its potential for the service of the Church both within and beyond the Diocese.

Archbishop Vincent spoke to us all at that meeting about the core mission of Maryvale – the mission to focus our teaching and our programmes of learning on the heart of the Church's faith and doctrine.

Over the last nine years this has continued to be his guiding principle. In addition, as a result of the very positive reports issuing from a number of validation events of both the Institute as a whole and

MISSIONARY FOR HUMAN ECOLOGY

Fr Peter Conley

PP The Mother of God and Guardian Angels, Castle Bromwich and Shard End

---

Mother of God and Guardian Angels, Castle Bromwich celebrates its diamond jubilee, 2007
Photographer: **Sue Conway**

Being asked by Archbishops, Bishops and others to comment on a range of matters is an occupational hazard for a priest with an STL who is also one of the 'Diocesan Censors of Books' (a title which is, perhaps, a distant echo of the Spanish Inquisition!).

Archbishop Vincent had only been in post a little while when he consulted me on a number of unrelated issues over a short period of time. Mindful of his skill in administration and the fact that neither he nor I knew each other that well, I thought it best to reply to him with individual letters.

We memorably matched each other and, nodding to his love of football, literally a '10-10 draw' resulted during one unforgettable two week period! I subsequently learned the wisdom of grouping my thoughts into fewer letters, much to his relief!

As a public speaker he has the capacity to inspire and I, among many, always looked forward to hearing him. The Archbishop was always encouraging of my theological interests and paid me the high compliment of incorporating my ideas on the importance of John Paul II's teaching on the 'ecological perspective' in his sermons, addresses and, in particular, the CES document 'Catholic Schools, Children of Other Faiths and Community Cohesion'.

In his speech to a conference on the Visions for Leadership in Catholic Education in March this year, Archbishop Nichols quoted the late Pope: 'The education which the Church promotes looks to the integral development of the human person. Its purpose is to cultivate the intellect and develop the capacity for right judgement, to help young people to assimilate their cultural heritage and form a sense of moral and ethical readiness for their future professional, civic, family and national responsibilities. An all-round education seeks to develop every aspect of the individual: social, intellectual, emotional, moral and spiritual. For there is an ecology of human growth which means that if any one of these elements is overlooked all the others suffer.'

During his time with us Archbishop Vincent faithfully sought to promote this ecological vision. ∎

SUPPORTING THE RELIGIOUS

Sr Thérèse Browne
Mother Superior
Sisters of Charity of St Paul
Selly Park

I can remember in early 2000 the sense of excitement and great hope among the religious of the diocese on hearing of the appointment of Archbishop Vincent as the next Archbishop of Birmingham. This sense of excitement and hope was combined also with wonder at what the appointment of this new, young and energetic Archbishop might mean for us and indeed the diocesan community as a whole.

During the intervening years we came to see that his leadership has always been from the front. He inspires confidence and displays great wisdom, together with a simple and deep spirituality rooted in his strong and firm faith. During his time with us he addressed many

HE HAS ALWAYS BEEN
GREATLY APPRECIATIVE OF
THE CONTRIBUTION MADE
BY RELIGIOUS TO THE
MISSION OF THE CHURCH
THROUGH OUR PRESENCE
AND THE RICH DIVERSITY
OF OUR MINISTRIES.

very difficult issues on behalf of the Catholic Community not just in Birmingham but also on a national level, and despite it all he did not lose either his youth or energy.

Archbishop Vincent has always been greatly appreciative of the contribution made by religious to the mission of the Church through our presence and the rich diversity of our ministries. We are deeply grateful to him too for his presence and support when it was needed and particularly for the trust he placed in us.

His new ministry in the Archdiocese of Westminster will, once again, take him to the front line in so many ways but we have no doubt that the God who has claims on him will bring to the forefront in a new and vigorous way his innate gifts of wisdom, courage and faith, which he needs to embrace in his new role with confidence, hope and joy.

Archbishop Vincent can be assured of the prayers, love and best wishes of the religious. We ask too for remembrance in his prayers.

As we bid you farewell we send you on your way with a blessing in the words of the late John O'Donohue:

'Awaken your spirit to adventure.
Hold nothing back,
learn to find ease in risk.
Soon you will be home
in a new rhythm,
for your soul senses the world that
awaits you.'
(Benedictus – A Book of Blessings)

THE GIFT OF DIALOGUE

Bill Ozanne
Secretary to the Diocesan Commission
for Inter-Religious Dialogue

No-one warns bishops that they will have to meet/deal with a constant stream of people each totally committed to their particular concern, and that they will have to switch on and off at half-hour intervals. When you met Archbishop Vincent you felt that his attention was fully engaged, whether you were a toddling visitor or an ancient pillar of the church.

Some snapshots include: Archbishop Vincent greeting the Annual Birmingham Inter-Faith Peace Walk about to set off at 8.30 on a damp July morning, or borrowing a straw hat to go into the Moseley Synagogue with the group another year. Then there was him sitting on the floor of the Clifton Road Shia prayer room at 6.30 a.m. to eat with the young Muslims after speaking at their Peace Vigil.

Third Bilateral Dialogue between Catholics and Sikhs held in Birmingham, 2008
Photographer: **Peter Jennings**

'HE WELCOMED WARMLY REPRESENTATIVES OF HINDU, BUDDHIST, SIKH, MUSLIM, JEWISH COMMUNITIES AS HONOURED GUESTS'

At the Civic Mass each year on the feast of Christ the King, he would warmly welcome as honoured guests representatives of Hindu, Buddhist, Sikh, Muslim and Jewish communities, along with civic dignitaries and the many papal knights.

He did not stint on these occasions on preaching about their civic responsibilities towards building Christ's kingdom of justice and peace. He was as ready to give personal support to the beleaguered parish of the Rosary in Saltley when they opened their Mariam House for inter-faith meetings.

One significant innovation was when he opened the 'Synod Hall' for the annual Clergy Day on Inter-Religious Dialogue, where up to 50 of the clergy gathered to hear major speakers on the current work of the Church in this area and to share their own problems and solutions. As Chair of the Birmingham Faith Leaders Group, he responded to an invitation to meet in the Central Mosque and then in the Guru Nanak Gurdwara in Handsworth. Underlying the discretion that goes with responsibility for what you say was the livewire that made him one of the cutting edge thinkers of the Pastoral Congress in Liverpool (his long-haired days!)

Westminster will provide its own demands and priorities, but while we miss him here, we can be sure that his continuing dialogue with people of other religions in this wider football pitch will be very fruitful. ∎

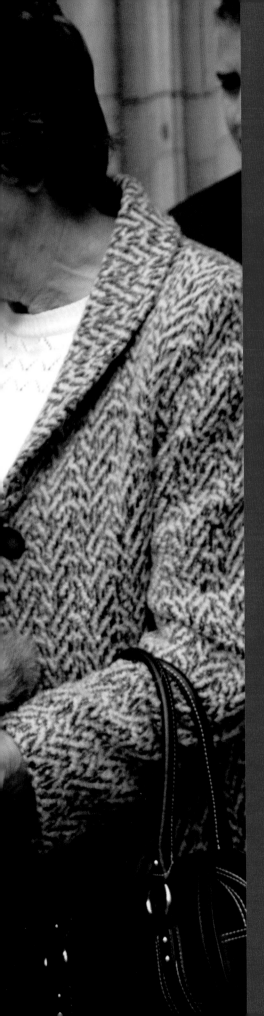

PICTURE GALLERY

Ordination of Fr Richard Sharples 2006
Photographer: **Sue Conway**

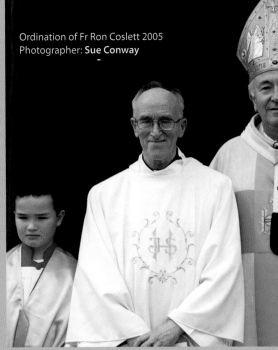

Ordination of Fr Ron Coslett 2005
Photographer: **Sue Conway**

Ordination of Fr Paul Haines 2006
Photographer: **Sue Conway**

Ordination of Fr Paul Smith 2008
Photographer: **Sue Conway**

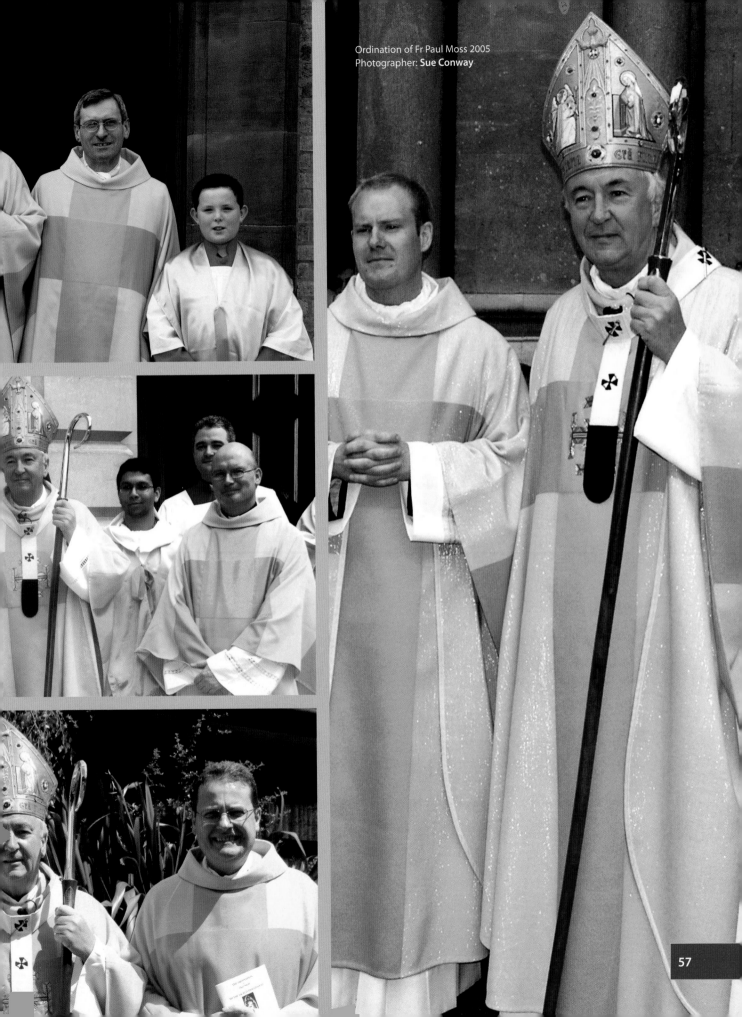

Ordination of Fr Paul Moss 2005
Photographer: **Sue Conway**

Releasing balloons with children from Blessed Teresa of Calcutta Primary School, Stafford, to celebrate the launch of Catholic Today in February 2005
Photographer: **Ed Moss**

Archbishop Vincent's charity fund-raising event for the Johnson Fund 2009

59

Polish Mass 2009
Photographer: Józef Łopuszyński

Easter Vigil 2006
Photographer: Sue Conway

Outside St Chad's 2006
Photographer: **Sue Conway**

Final Mass at St Chad's Cathedral 2009
Photographer: **Sue Conway**

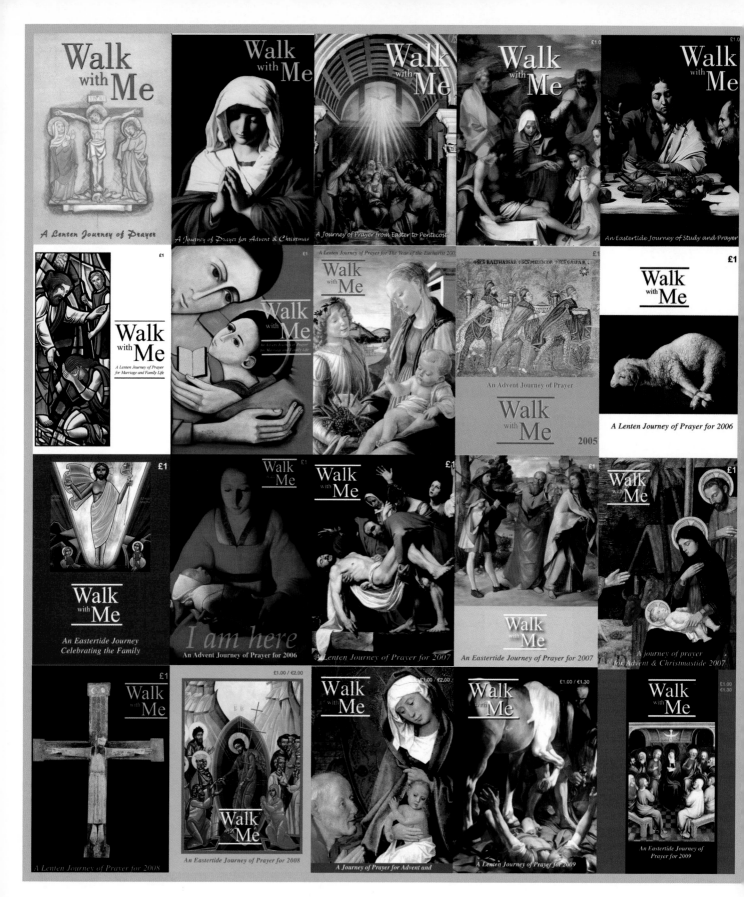

Walk with Me the popular seasonal prayer and scripture booklet is the inspiration of Archbishop Vincent. Launched in 2001 by Alive Publishing, it has now been taken up by many other dioceses and has an overall circulation throughout Advent, Lent and Easter of 600,000.

St John Fisher's Altar Servers, West Heath 2006
Photographer: **Sue Conway**

Altar Servers' Mass at St Chad's Cathedral 2007
Photographer: **Sue Conway**

Ubi Caritas Awards 2005
Photographer: **Sue Conway**

WELCOME
to the
Metropolitan Cathedral
of St Chad

Mother Church of the
Roman Catholic
Archdiocese of Birmingham

Consecrated 21 June 1841

Minor Basilica
11 June 1941

Archbishop Vincent with St Chad's
Primary School, Final Mass 2009
Photographer: **Sue Conway**

Holy Thursday 2009
Photographer: Sue Conway

66

Archbishop Vincent meets Fernando Torres
Photographer: **Peter Jennings**

Anfield 2009

In his garden at Archbishop's House, Birmingham
Picture by **Peter McDonald**

In his garden at Archbishop's House, Birmingham
Picture by **Peter Nichols**

On the ferry to Straddie
Picture by **Peter Nichols**

Sydney Airport
Picture by **Peter Nichols**

Archbishop Vincent with his two
brothers Peter and John
Photographer: Peter Jennings

Peter Jennings
*Press Secretary to
Archbishop Vincent Nichols, as
Archbishop of Birmingham, 2000-09*

SEVEN MAGIC MOMENTS

I first met Vincent Nichols in Rome in September 1980 when I was covering the Synod on Marriage and the Family. I was introduced to him outside the Pope VI Synod Hall by Cardinal Basil Hume OSB and Archbishop Derek Worlock of Liverpool. Fr Basil, as we knew him, said: 'This is Fr Vincent Nichols. He's here to help us. I think you'll like him'.

Nearly twenty-nine years later I felt extremely proud as I sat in Westminster Cathedral at his Reception and Installation as the Eleventh Archbishop of Westminster.

I have seven 'magic moments' to share from that historic ceremony on Thursday 21 May 2009. It has been an honour to serve my dear friend Vincent Nichols as his Press Secretary during his time as Archbishop of Birmingham. I was available 24/7 to advise, help, and do my best to ensure he received appropriate profile and positive media coverage.

The installation was a moving, prayerful and memorable occasion. The Votive Mass of Saint Paul the Apostle was full of ancient tradition and ritual, some dating back to the earliest days of Christianity in Britain. But there were also delightful unscripted and unscheduled moments which will remain with me as never-to-be-repeated 'magic moments'.

I think first of the 'thumbs up' that Archbishop Vincent gave to his brother John, who was sitting in a wheelchair directly in front of the pulpit. This delightful picture was captured by the Press Association photographer Fiona Hanson, with whom I had worked in Gibraltar on a project to produce the world's fastest postage stamp in April 2001.

This picture was released by the Press Association who, forgivably, had not grasped its significance. Those of us seated near to John saw what actually happened, an intimate family moment between two brothers as the new Archbishop processed from the sanctuary at the end of the two-hour service.

My second 'magic moment' was when I first picked up the beautifully produced service booklet and saw my own colour picture of Archbishop Vincent Nichols on the inside of the front cover. It was not captioned but I had pictured Westminster's new man outside the Metropolitan Cathedral and Basilica of St Chad, Birmingham. He was wearing the vestments and mitre of his great predecessor, Bishop William Bernard Ullathorne, OSB, first Bishop of Birmingham, 1850-1888.

My third 'magic moment' was when Archbishop Vincent stepped up to the microphone in the pulpit to deliver his sermon. It was good to see him up there; pulpits are somewhat undersused these days. I caught his eye and waved, and he flashed back one of his characteristic, meaningful smiles that I came to know so well during my nine years' work at his side.

My fourth 'magic moment' was when Archbishop Nichols was handed the crozier, the sign of the Shepherd of the Flock, by his predecessor Cardinal Cormac Murphy-O'Connor. Some in the congregation, like myself, smiled, because it had been Bishop Nichols, then Apostolic Administrator of the Archdiocese of Westminster, who had handed Cardinal Basil Hume's crozier to Bishop Cormac during the latter's Mass of Installation as the Archbishop of Westminster in Westminster Cathedral, on 22 March 2000.

Pope John Paul II had appointed Bishop Cormac Murphy-O'Connor of Arundel and Brighton as the tenth Archbishop of Westminster on 21 February that year. Cardinal Murphy-O'Connor is the first Archbishop of Westminster to live into retirement, and thus the first to hand over his crozier to a successor Archbishop.

My fifth 'magic moment' was when Chris Nichols, the Archbishop's sister-in-law, read the first lesson and Jenny Davies read the second lesson. Chris and Peter Nichols had flown over from Australia to be with their brother for this most important ceremony. Mrs Jennifer Davies, who was his personal secretary for all the years he was Archbishop of Birmingham, had also worked for the late Archbishop Couve de Murville when he was Archbishop of Birmingham prior to Vincent Nichols; long service indeed.

My sixth 'magic moment' was watching the new Archbishop of Westminster warmly greet the Archbishop of Canterbury, Dr Rowan Williams and the now Archbishop of York, Dr John Sentamu. Archbishop Vincent had worked closely with Bishop John Sentamu and other faith leaders in Birmingham. As Anglican Bishop of Stepney, John Sentamu had attended Archbishop Vincent's Installation in the Metropolitan Cathedral and Basilica of St Chad Birmingham in March 2000. John Sentamu later became Anglican Bishop of Birmingham and forged a real bond there with Archbishop Nichols.

My seventh 'magic moment' happened as Archbishop Vincent was processing from the sanctuary at the end of the two-hour-plus service before making his way out into the warm afternoon sunshine to greet the crowds gathered in the piazza. With simple solemnity, and completely off the schedule, he turned and entered the Chapel of St Gregory and St Augustine near the great West Door of Westminster Cathedral.

There he paused for a few moments to kneel and pray before the tomb of his great friend and mentor Cardinal Basil Hume. Cardinal Basil Hume, OSB, OM, died on 17 June 1999, aged 76. At the conclusion of the funeral in Westminster Cathedral on Friday 25 June that year, it was Bishop Vincent Nichols who walked before Fr Basil's coffin and led it to its final resting place.

After that first introduction in Rome I followed all the major milestones in Vincent Nichol's ecclesiastical career. He has always been affectionately referred to as 'Vin'. In January 1984, he was appointed General Secretary of the Bishops' Conference in England and Wales. Pope John Paul II appointed Mgr Vincent as an Auxiliary Bishop in the Archdiocese of Westminster on 5 November 1991. He was aged 46, and at the time the youngest Catholic bishop in Great Britain.

His Episcopal Ordination took place in Westminster Cathedral on 24 January 1992, the feast of St Francis de Sales, Patron of Writers and Journalists. He was given responsibility for North London. His patch included the old Wembley Stadium where supporters sang 'Football's Coming Home' during Euro 96.

Today, Vincent Gerard Nichols, the lad from Liverpool, has come back to London as Archbishop of Westminster, now assuming the care of the whole diocese, and, as the newly elected President of the Catholic Bishops' Conference of England and Wales. May Westminster be his home for many years to come!■

Installation of Archbishop Vincent at Westminster
Picture courtesy of Public Affairs Office, Diocese of Westminster